Destiny's Fight

A "Grab that Gift Series"

by

Christiana .T. Moronfolu

Order this book online at www.trafford.com
or email orders@trafford.com

Most Trafford titles are also available at major online book retailers.

COVER DESIGN BY
TBIC
Batonoflove_ventures@yahoo.com

TYPE SETTING BY
Trafford Publishers

BIBLE REFERENCE
New King James Version (NKJV)

REVISED STANDARD VERSION
COPYRIGHT © 1971 BY COLLINS BIBLE

The bible quotations are from Ilumina DVD.

Printed in the United States of America.

ISBN: 978-1-4669-5457-1 (sc)
ISBN: 978-1-4669-5458-8 (e)

Trafford rev. 09/25/2012

 www.trafford.com

North America & international
toll-free: 1 888 232 4444 (USA & Canada)
phone: 250 383 6864 ♦ fax: 812 355 4082

CONTENTS

ACKNOWLEDGEMENT:

With sincere gratitude and appreciation:

- *To my parents, my siblings and their spouses and all the children: I say thank you for providing the foundational support that helped me grow into all God has for me. You made me believe in myself and appreciate all God has done in my life. The word of God from your mouths has kept me standing tall, after the numerous trials and storms. I would never forget the love God allowed you to show me.*

- *To all ministers of God, who labour in His vineyard, to ensure that we get the finest of the wheat, I say a big thank you to you. Thank you for your obedience to God's word, and thank you for looking after God's children. Like the rod of Moses (backed by the word of God), it is amazing what a sermon directed by God can do. Thank you for all your life-transforming and healing sermons.*

- *To all my mentors in the market place and all those who love to see others succeed the way God wants them to, I say thank you. You make the difference in the kingdom of God. You were the ones I saw and made up my mind to always seek God in all I do. You showed me what was possible if I can dare to pursue my God in the market place. Your hands would never lack the support from God in Jesus' name.*

- *To all my other good friends, colleagues and family members. I do not think I could have succeeded without God bringing me into your lives. I saw the hand of God in you, and knew that I was fortunate to have come into your lives. Thank you for the race you have run with me and we thank God for the tracks that lie ahead of us. It has been challenging, but enjoyable. We thank God for the sweet fellowship we enjoy in the presence of the Holy Spirit. Thank you for all your love and support in the journey so far.*

My Glazed Kettle:
It does not break,
When subjected to heat.

See the unbeatable make,
All elegantly lit.

That's how it takes
All the extreme heat,
And only releases,
Colourful spectra of steam,
That teases my eyes.

Be like my glazed kettle,
In times of heat,
Amidst your fight,
Do all it takes,
To tease our eyes.

*"*F*ight the good fight,*
With all thy might,
Christ is thy strength,
And Christ thy might
Lay hold on life,
And it shall be,
Thy joy and crown eternally".

-John Samuel Bewley Monsell (1811-1875)

The house of creativity
Philippians 3 vs. 20 *"For our citizenship is in heaven, from which we eagerly wait for the Saviour, the Lord Jesus Christ"*.

FROM THE AUTHOR:
ONE GOD, ONE YOU, ONE ME

1st Corinthians 12 vs.12 *"For as the body is one and has many members, but all the members of that one body, being many, are one body, so also is Christ".*

There is a fight God has called us to engage in, because not all fights are profitable and not all guarantee victory. There is however one that you owe yourself to win. It is the greatest gift you can bestow on your person. It is the fight to live. Life can be a challenge, if you do not fight for your right to live. From the moment a baby is born, you can see the tiny fight—grasping the first breathe, trying to feed, and fighting for independence. The fight does not stop until such an individual breathes his last. To fight is to live.

More so, there are battles that are personal and some that are corporate. Overcoming the personal fights most times is key to overcoming the corporate ones and you need to distinguish between the two. At creation, according to Genesis, God made you in His image (holiness and gave you the ability to take charge of your life with its challenges). We also know that He is one, you are one and I am one. An understanding of these uniqueness is not automatic if you do not press in, you would win your battles. When you understand your uniqueness, you would learn how to fight and win.

In addition, the bible talks about the body—that is the church of the living God, being one, race, tribe, age and sex. God's will is to see us all in heaven at the end of our journey here on earth. Then we would have served God, and fought the fight of life. That is what qualifies us to be citizens of heaven. Although this is the truth, we all have our different functions or roles to play. This is why Paul advised Timothy not to forget his gift. God was going to use him and his gift to reach out to others and get them into the kingdom as well. 1st Timothy 4 vs.14.

More so, being in the company of others can help certain gifts manifest, as some cannot function well in isolation. You may have certain gifts, and it may take a conscious effort to remember them. It is tragedy to forget your gifts because it means forgetting that you can be a blessing. Whether, individual or corporate, you must appreciate God, as your creator, and men; as His creation. A way to look at this is to see heaven as our common destination in God; and a mansion (where we will all end up). This would make it easier to integrate people and be integrated.
John 14vs.2

Jesus has already gone ahead of us to prepare a place for every one who belongs to Him. Who are those who belong to Him? As long as you accept God, you belong to His household; this makes us all neighbours and housemates — brothers and sisters. Life is a journey filled with challenges (roadblocks) and our bodies are vehicles that go through life. Every now and again, we may encounter these challenges, and their magnitude and nature may range from being physical, emotional, financial and psychological to being spiritual. For ease of reading and to help you capture an image of 'fellowship in heaven', I have referred to your sphere of influence as "your house mates". As citizens of heaven, we would all belong to one house; God — the house or embodiment of creativity. As an art based person, I love journeys, and I take delight in feeling every moment of my day. However, the Holy Spirit said to me one morning; "Life is a teacher that must teach". Either you learn from experience, or you become one of her students. There are some lectures that you do not need to attend". This made a lot of sense to me, because we can all learn from one another's experiences. Time is not enough to experience all on ones own. Fasten your seat belts. Relax. Take a deep breathe. Enjoy the book.

THE INTRODUCTION:

Genesis 14vs. 11 '*And when the vultures came down on the carcasses, Abram drove them away*'

Destiny's fight" is a book that aids your fight for life. It gives you a reason to stay alive. It helps you understand that living is your right, and to choose not to live makes one less of the person God intends one to be. As you read along, you would identify your individuality or uniqueness in God and be motivated to fight for your destiny. You'ld discover how you can live a successful life. It is not just about seeking Jesus Christ, it is looking at others through Him. It is serving Him. This may require a fight sometimes.

Yes. Sometime, you may have to fight to serve God. In the scripture above, when Abram presented his offering to God, as instructed, the vultures came visiting. God knew that the vultures were aiming for the offering, and He left Abram to his discretion. Thank God, Abram drove the ravenger away. 'What if I do not have a reason to fight or I can't find my place in the scheme of things'? Well living can be a torment if you find it hard to place yourself in the environment, let alone have something to fight for. When this happens, the opportunity to serve is almost impossible. Therefore, you need to fight to identify your place in life. How do I fight to serve or stay alive?

If you are asking these questions, this book is for you. God interrupted me, just to share the joy of being alive with you. God told me to stop, so you can move ahead. Do you know a place called "dead" when you are still alive? I have been there, and I do not wish go back again. God wants you out of there too. He wants those of you who are in the midst of personal challenges that have the potential to mar or reduce your level of productivity. He wants us to fight for our destiny. Your destiny wants you to fight for her, and influence generations to come. This is when it becomes glorious.

It is also for you if you or your loved ones find it difficult to stay conscious (alive). It would also inspire those who would rather be unconventional and still make ends meet. "Destiny's fight" encapsulates actual life experiences, which can proffer ways of alleviating certain fears associated with personal development and growth. Here you learn to take charge of your life and destiny, draw closer to God, boost your morale and encourage a safer, healthier and more beautiful environment that you would be proud to be a part.

Lastly, I would be referring to the book of Genesis, as it contains the story of creation — the beginning of man, the beginning of his fall and the beginning of God's restoration plan. What better time is it to begin to take ownership of your life than now? What better time is it to begin to serve God than now? What better time is it to begin to fight until you leave a landmark than now?

1

ENCAPSULATION OF DESTINY

Exodus 28vs.3 *"So you shall speak to all who are gifted artisans, whom I have filled with the spirit of wisdom . . . ."*

Destiny refers to an expected future or end of a matter or an individual. It is the summation or encapsulation of man's life. What you want at the end of the day is a glorious destiny. Can we talk about this without the one who controls it? Not really. God is the embodiment of a glorious destiny. If we want a glorious destiny, we need to explore the totality of God. You cannot know it all, but as you seek Him, He would give you what is sufficient for your existence. In your pursuit for destiny, you also need to understand that God has all the attributes that make Him reliable, even in the face of uncertainty. He has neatly wrapped up packets of exciting opportunities yet to be discovered, which evolve with time and development. This is what creativity is all about.

Creativity refers to the art of being imaginative, resourceful, and inventive. It is the originality of a thing, idea, or concept and is seen in all spheres of life. The principle of creation is illustrated in Genesis 1 and God has since passed the baton of creativity to man. Although man received this baton, he still needs to look up to the Creator, for inspiration and guidance. The reason for this is so that he can successfully capture his ideas through his mind; the conduit of creativity and birth them. The creator; God, being a spirit, does not have a physical brain like man, yet He instigates all divine ideas. He is thus the source; and embodiment or house of creativity. He is the one who energises and controls man's destiny. Just like there are several rooms in some houses, in the house of creativity, there is an ever-flowing source of creativity. This flows in to man's mind and controls his intellectual capacity (brain), and ultimately his destiny.

More so, the thought process known to man is the one that he has decided to term normal. He has thus designed his environment taking into account all that is normal. Perhaps one of the things he did not receive was the full details of the master plan of his future. This is what differentiates man from his maker, and this has been one of his fights to date. The fight to be the 'supreme creator' rather than a housemate from the "house of creativity". Having limited God to only what he knows, man has fought everything unusual, neglected, and abused God's other creation. This is illustrated in Acts 11 vs. 6-10. Peter had always known certain animals as being unclean. Even when God gave him the permission to eat of it, his paradigm would not take it. Peter could only see the unclean animal; he could not see the succulent flesh! Acts 11 vs.6-10.

More so, recently God has shocked man by allowing him to see that there are people whose approach to life is slightly different to the ones he is aware. He once called it an abnormality, but today; he is now agreeing with God that it is not. It is a "God — way" of demonstrating His transcendent powers — through the most unlikely people, using the most unlikely methods. I hear God calling you if you have ever been classified as a nonentity or non-achiever. I hear God calling you if you suspect you miraculously escaped the classification. I hear God calling parents who have children who have been classified under these groups. Creation is waiting for you. Creation is waiting for your child. Creation is waiting for the manifestations of God's children. Romans 8 vs. 19.

Creation also involves envisioning the abstract and skilful planning in order to convert the abstract into reality. We have seen these works of creativity carried out by men the world considered "right". Well I am happy to announce that creation is waiting for the creativity from those who the world seems to have "left behind"; those with god-hidden talents that are evolving.

People may call you a psychologically challenged person, but you are not. That is not how God classifies you. Agreed you may have uncommon abilities, but this is because of the undiscovered truths, which is found in God, the house of creativity and encapsulation of men's destiny. If you can unravel Him, through His word, you would discover some hints about your destiny. His word is like a maze that you go through to unravel your identity and destiny.

Do not fight God, He knows who you are. The more you fight God, the less likely you are to discover the truth that has been around for a long time — your god given creative ability. You may have been classified with a challenge, which may even be obvious, but this is only man's way of responding to your condition. God is different. When He looks at you, He sees His paragon of perfection, suitable for His glory and purpose. Release yourself to Him. Allow Him to reveal your true identity to you. Presently you may even have dreams that transcend your reach. You may even have been told in times past "if you can think it, then you can have it", but now having thought all you know to think, you feel like your dreams can only materialise in your mind. Do not worry; God is able to turn your dreams into reality. The more you expose yourself to the one who knows the future, the more of Him you know, and the more He blesses your memory — retentive capability. **Proverbs 10 vs.7** *"The memory of the righteous is blessed . . . .".*

How ever, for God to do this, you must acknowledge Him as the source of your inspiration; your reservoir of knowledge and the, the house of creativity. May be the reason why you have not attained those dreams is because it is "a dream'. In Exodus **31 vs.3-5,** God said He has poured

Creation is waiting for you. Creation is waiting for your child.

out His creative spirit into you. It is time to leave the dream world and begin to live up to the expectations of creation. Begin to take advantage of your unique learning abilities to co-operate with God and reveal the truths that are still hidden. The dream world is good, but it can be bad if you never leave it. You need to come out of it and explore your ideas. Proverbs 20 vs.13. For Abraham to step into all that God had for him, he had to leave Lot (his brother in law) behind. For you, your Lot could be your dream world. Ideas can only become a reality when it is explored. Genesis 13 vs.14-17. Try all you can to make your dreams come to live.

Finally, since God is the house of creativity, the One who gives ability to all men, He will have the final say in your life. There is a clarion call from God, the house of creativity. Hand your affairs over to the Encapsulation of your destiny.

Watch Him fine-tune you into the creative genius. Walk with Him to your glorious future. Allow Him use you to influence His kingdom for good.

2

BLOCKS OF DESTINY

1 Chronicles 22vs.2 *'So David gave orders to call together the foreigners living in Israel, and he assigned them the task of preparing blocks of stone for building the temple of God'.*

The erection of every building starts with laying the blocks from the foundation; the same applies to man's destiny. Blocks of destiny are the essential elements for building a strong future. For you to have a bright one, you must lay the right blocks. It is not enough for you to know the encapsulation of a glorious destiny; you need to also learn from Him. As you wait on Him, He would hand down to you the right blocks to lay for your future. In the end, your life would be like an edifice; moulded by the one who I choose to call "the house of creativity". You do not have to be in 'your space' to begin to build. David in the verse quoted above assigned tasks to the foreigners; and this was not optional. Infact under the old covenant, the foreigner that joined himself with Israel was compelled to 'serve' the God of Israel. Numbers 9 vs.14.

In the previous chapter, we considered God, the source of all creativity and man; a medium through which He continues His work. This means that you have the right to receive your own blocks from God and begin creating what you want your future to be. God would not set you on a course without a mandate or instruction. In Genesis, He thought of you, before he issued the command to be fruitful. Make sure you understand it before setting out. We know from 1st Corinthians 12 vs.12 that God is one, and since you are created in His image, you are also one. Your personal acceptance is there fore a fundamental block you need to start building your glorious future or destiny. This is what I would be focusing on in this chapter.

Bearing this in mind, we would therefore be looking at your uniqueness and the mandate of God on you. The first command God gave man in Eden is that of productivity and dominion. Both require the use of your creativity. The expected end of all creativity is productivity. To be productive there fore, you need a plan, not just any plan; you need God's plan and idea. To refuse this mandate, or block of destiny is to disobey God. It is not a choice to be considered, it is a mandate — an instruction from above. Be creative — *produce . . . multiply . . . . replenish . . .*" If He did not put the creative gene to accomplish this in you, He would not have issued the command. You only invest in people you are concerned about; this is what God did in Genesis, before giving the mandate. Remember He cares for you and your plans. It is not burdensome to Him. He does this joyfully. This is the only way that your creativity can be released. Zephaniah 3 vs.17, Matthew 10vs. 31.

God first loved you, before calling you to fulfil the task or mandate. You need to be aware of your uniqueness, before you can reach out to the mandate to be creative. Understanding your uniqueness — what makes you stand out as an individual is another building block. God has placed a value on you that cost Him His blood (Son). That is love. In return, you need to love and accept yourself, so you can celebrate the person God has made you to be. It is when you get to this point, that you would be able to appreciate God genuinely, and this will motivate you to strive to be in His will. As a child, I saw one of Napoleon's inscription on a wall and it read: "*what you are is God's gift to you, and what you make of yourself is your gift to God*".

More so, you cannot keep blaming your circumstances, and refuse to progress. At some stage, you must straighten up and take responsibility for every thing that pertains to you (including your circle of influence). I remember one constant line my mother used to recite in my local dialect, while I was growing up: "a child must transform himself". God wants you to appreciate you; in fact, He calls you a crown of beauty and a royal diadem. You are a precious gem, and you know what a precious gem does for its owner. It is mandated to bring out its owner's attraction. You are mandated to bring out the glory of God on earth, through your works. Isaiah 62 vs.3. He does not want others to define you, because His word has already done that. This implies that you must agree with His word concerning you. Job 22 vs.21

However, for some of you, the inability to appreciate yourself may stem from the fact that you are aware of certain undesirable traits within your lineage, which is now manifesting in your life. Although you carry your parents' genes, you are not your parents. Do not despise yourself when you see yourself exhibiting certain traits you disliked in your parents. Embrace yourself and thank God, at least the traits confirm your identity with your parents. There are those who are not sure about this, or who were not privileged to know their biological parents. My prayer for them is that they would find their identity in God, since He is the Father of all. I want you to know that God still loves you and He wants you to know that He cares for you more than any human being would. To those without love, He remains THE PARENT — El-Shaddai — all sufficient one. Ephesians 4vs.6

However, the unfavourable traits you discovered should be used as a tool for learning how to identify with, understand, and relate to your authority figures. It is very easy to despise authority figures and your house mates for the things they do, until you find yourself doing likewise. I am not suggesting that you condone the

"Allow God use it to heal you of all negative emotions acquired from childhood".

negatives in your life; but you use it as a tool to connect with and understand the reason behind certain actions.

Allow God use it to heal you of all negative emotions acquired from childhood. Celebrate the good ones and ask God to help you to deal with the bad ones . . . . seek for help if necessary. Interestingly enough, since God made us all in His image, we tend to react to things in a similar way, when exposed to similar conditions. The principle of empathy (a mind game, which involves role switch) is this, if you put people in your shoes, you would be able to connect and work together with them.

Once the motive behind the action has been realised, and found to have produced a poor out come, then it will be wise to seek other ways of approaching similar situations, should there be a repeat performance in your life. Having said this, there would be times when you would fall short in this area that is not the time to condemn yourself. Do not let your past control you, by dwelling on it. I saw an inscription recently *"the most you can do about your past is to leave it alone"*. The only time when your past is good in the present is if you can use it to create a wealth of blessings for others to glean from. A biblical example of someone who did not allow his past or lineage to deter him was Saul, who later became Paul. Today he would be considered as a serial killer; killing Christians. However, after his conversion, he left his past alone and did not allow any one take him there. He went further to declare the following: Galatians 6vs.17. Remember one thing; you are not perfect, neither is anyone.

Lastly, only God can claim ultimate perfection, so do not allow people to bury you with criticism. Hear the voice of Jesus from your grave, let the Spirit of God anoint you with the oil of resurrection, and let the restoring arms of Jesus raise you high above the storms of life. This is the only way

God can make all things work together to your advantage, and for His glory. Romans 8 vs.28.

Therefore, I beseech you; arise to your uniqueness in God. Arise to your unique gift, (ability), and be creative. Arise, take those blocks and begin to build.

3

THE FIGHT

2nd Timothy 4vs.7 *'I have fought a good fight, I have finished my course, I have kept the faith'*

THe day you begin to understand and appreciate the God in you, is the day you would receive the strength to fight for your destiny. This is a gift God has given and as you deplore it, others would be blessed. To fight is to contend for a favourable result. Creativity is a fight in itself. It is a fight against normalcy, in order to improve the performance of what exists. Having received the instruction to be creative (be a blessing to others), you need to find how and where this can happen best.

The command has being given, and you know the One who issued it. Now you need to identify where you fit and how you fit. This may appear easy and straight forward, what makes it tricky is the fact that everybody can find where they fit, but not everyone can fit where they find. You as an individual have a role to play, which no one else can. Unless you arise and begin to take responsibility for your gifts, and its application, you may not find a place for yourself in life. Where information on your life or destiny is inadequate, get involved with others who are threading on similar path. Remember God is the God of knowledge. Fight to be educated on matters regarding your endeavour. 1st Samuel 2 vs.3

In addition to this personal knowledge, you should learn your culture, keep your tradition, but do not allow it hinder your creativity. This is because the system of governance of any advancing society has creativity at its nerve centre. Willingness to carry out, explore and transfer knowledge through documentation is what makes these nations grow. You need to be diligent about your dream, for your uniqueness to be accepted to all. Your diligence can be seen in your fight. 2nd Timothy 2 vs.15.

However, if you will fight for your call to uniqueness, you have to be ready for the journey that lies ahead. It is challenging, but so is life. What is not worth fighting for is not worth living for. Regardless of the nature of the fight, you would require patience. It may take time, which if you are willing to give to the Encapsulation of your Destiny (God), will produce a harvest of blessings to you and your generations to come. You have to answer the call yourself; you cannot afford to allow someone else answer the call for you. It is a call to display your uniqueness. A fight to remain alive in the midst of competition from others.

More so, as you learn more about your fights and challenges, be determined to do something about it. For what you cannot change, God would send help your way. Remember, it was only when Adam became busy in the garden that God sent help his way. Get up and do something. Genesis 2 vs.8, Genesis 2 vs.20-22. Your fight here is to try your best to be busy for God — not only in ministry or church, but also in the market place — your circular work or school. Fight to listen to Him, as He speaks to you personally through the word, or through others. Fight to serve Him. As you do this, He would meet your needs according to His riches in glory. You need to press in, until you get the desired result. Philippians 4vs.19, Philippians 3 vs.14.

> Learn more about your challenges and be determined to do something about it.

Another reason why you have to fight to be busy for God is this, as you become busy, you will begin to identify exactly where you need help. When God sends the help(s), you will not take undue advantage of them. Rather, you would be prepared to work with them, and show the help(s) the area you want them to assist. If you do not want to hurt those whom God has sent your way, then rise up and do something.

More so, fight for your talent to become useful and experiment your ideas, paint, draw, sing, dance, read, e.t.c. You can fight to be educated by submitting to the necessary training required to attain the knowledge desired. 2nd Peter 2 vs.15. If learning is a setback, start where you are; even if it means spending hours on a page. Find out about the different styles of learning, and pick the one you prefer most. Remember, you are the only one that can see your dream; others would only join to strengthen you. The success is therefore dependent on how much you are willing to invest in it to make it materialise.

Fight for your uniqueness. Fight to be discovered as a positive contributor. Fight for the glory of God to be revealed through you.

4

THE WRESTLING RING

Nehemiah 4vs.20 "When you hear the blast of the trumpet, rush to wherever it is sounding. Then our God will fight for us'.

The wrestling ring is a designated platform where fights take place. In the fight for destiny, the platform could be a physical platform; at home, or society or even the market place. At home, it may be the wrestling ring of your finances, marital destiny or your child's future. In the society, the wrestling ring could be your studies, or just wrestling with the system and the way it works. The platform could also be a spiritual platform, in your mind. The mind is a platform where you struggle with changes, choices, and contemplations. The wrestling ring of your mind influences the daily decisions you make; which ultimately influences your destiny.

The wrestling ring at the market place could be performing a difficult task, relating with a fastidious colleague, or even attending certain meetings or social functions. Before you go to the wrestling ring, you need to know what part you would play. Depending on the fight in your life, you can be the fighter; fighting directly for your destiny, or the referee, settling the fight to get to your destiny. This means that you need to take a stand on competing choices. For example, you ought to settle your inner struggle (fight) between what churches to attend, which career choices to pursue, which schools to send your children to, how to manage your house mates, e.t.c. Exodus 2 vs.13. In the wrestling ring of your mind, you may also need to settle the fight by leaning on God and allowing Him fight for you. Exodus 14 vs.14.

Like every other activity, you need to be familiar with your environment to be able to apply yourself accordingly. Unless you know the ring well, you may be disqualified in the fight, even if you win. Genesis 26 vs. 16-23. As with every other sport, in a wrestling match, the wrestlers are encouraged to practice in the ring or a similar one, and get used to it, before the day of the event. Before you fight, ensure that you are conscious of the environment and know it well. Be sure that the rings of defence are in place, in firm position and the ground is safe enough for the fight. In the fight for destiny, you cannot afford to fight the battle like someone in a strange land, fight with discernment (in God).

As earlier stated, the fight for destiny begins from the cradle to the grave. When God created the world, He did not create it to be in chaos. Isaiah 45vs.18. Anytime you find an aspect of your life is heading for a chaotic mess, it is a battle cry; indicating that it is time to go onto the wrestling field. As you yield, to the word of God for directions you cannot go wrong in your fights. Nehemiah 4 vs.20.

More so, there are times and seasons of life. There is a time to fight and a time to rest. As you stay in tune with life, you would discern the time to take the appropriate action. There is also a time to fight for your mind, when the devil is trying to mess you up mentally, and there is also a time to fight for your career. There is a time to fight for your spiritual growth, so you do not miss the mark. There is also the time to fight for your marital destiny. All this happen according to God's timing. Fighting according to God's timing assures you of His victory, fighting in your own timing brings the reverse.

More so, to win the fight, you must know where the wrestling bout is. If it is your finances, where exactly is the wrestling ring? Is it in your spending habits, or your earning potentials? Do you need to evaluate your spending habit and be more disciplined? Do you need to apply yourself to fresh skills or change your job, to boost your earning potentials? If your mind is running amok, what area of your life is influencing this state of mind? Search for it and address it with the word of God. Where you need external help, do not hesitate to reach out for it, before it escalates. Exodus 1 vs.10.

In conclusion, make sure you identify your wrestling ring. Know when it is time to go to the ring. Go to the ring determined to win.

5

FIGHT ATTRIBUTES

1ˢᵗ Thessalonians 5vs.6 *"So be on your guard, not asleep like the others. Stay alert and be sober'*

K nowing fully well that the fight can take place anywhere, and at any time, you would need to be prepared to win every battle of your lives. As a child, in brownie, and red cross, we were told to: 'Be prepared always'. The sayings, 'To fail to plan, is to plan to fail', 'Proper preparation prevents poor performance' and 'Success depends on how high you set your standards', all point to the need to prepare well if you must succeed in your endeavours. Looking at 'destiny's fight' or better put 'life's battles' we cannot under estimate the need for you to be victorious. Remember, God gave you the power to dominate and rule your life and destiny, and His word is the guarantee that this is possible. Genesis 1vs. 28, Psalm 9vs.6.

Going back to 'your fight', remember also the saying 'a stitch in time saves nine'. This talks about taking precautionary steps to avoid or minimise a negative outcome. In the fight for destiny, part of taking precautionary measures is to identify root causes and arrest them before they escalate and become uncontrollable. Like we are already aware, although we are members of one household; God, we have differing abilities. Being able to identify with and respond positively to one another would help in winning life's battles. God made some housemates to be quick thinkers, with well-organised thought patterns. He also made some to be quick thinkers, with thoughts that run ahead of them. The early manifestations of this is 'confusion'. God made these housemates, but He is not the author of confusion.

If this describes you, God has already made a way out to help you combat this; all He asks you to do is to be patient and wait for Him and take time to be thorough in your preparations for success. This attribute should not be frowned upon. I guess God allows us to get to our destinations at different times to maintain a balance on life and foster continuity. Imagine if all your age mates in the world get married on the same day, there would be no weddings to attend on other days. That is extreme, but think of other events happening simultaneously and you'ld get the gist. Ecclesiastes 9vs.11.

Some housemates can also come across as being selfish due to internalisation. It may mean that they need more time to comprehend and process information than others. Accept them. It may also be that they are just self-centred. If you are the one that loves to internalise, make sure you ask for wisdom to balance your thought life. An imbalanced thought life can leave you with a distorted view of yourself or situation. May be this is why the bible says we should bear one another's burdens. As you concentrate more on others, you spend less time on yourself. Remember, Abraham looked out for Lot, despite Lot's greed and got blessed. As you look out for your housemates, God will look out for you. Genesis 13vs.10-13.

In addition, the down side to excessive internalisation could lead to obsession, which may manifest as a social handicap. This may make integration a challenge. Overcoming this habit may not be as easy as you would expect. Try it. When you or some of your housemates find it hard to blend in the environment, strengthen the support for one another by taking charge. Take the lead in breaking the ice. This is an aspect of growing up; and it certainly has its challenges, and could produce many anxieties as you become more aware of your uniqueness (vulnerability) and that of your housemates. The temptation here is to decline the invitation to take responsibility for anything because of this susceptibility. Where your motive is to achieve a unified system, or build a team, make sure you do not take undue advantage and make sure you are not taken for granted either.

Occasionally, you may also meet some housemates who are alive but not alert. It may be a compulsive behaviour and you only have to pray that the object of their focus is positive and godly. Like obsession, it involves being excessively attached to a thing and this translates into a continuous activity, which could be remarkable (positive or negative). Most times, this group of housemates may never bring you into their world, unless they trust you. When they do, access to vital parts maybe denied until an invitation is issued. This can be disturbing if it is a way of life, especially where it is counter productive.

A good sign in helping to identify if your housemates belong to this group described above is to observe their mannerism, and their attitude to work. Do they spend a lot of time doing a particular task? In performing this task, it is quite possible their brain is also busy trying to figure the way round the task. When interrupted, how do they react? The moment you begin to intervene with the natural pattern of their thoughts, the intervention is sensed as an irritation, and this will inevitably produce rebellion. So how do you manage and control this?

Where the obsession is influencing them to behave negatively, you must encourage your housemates to trade the object of obsession for a more positive one. For example, an obsession with stealing — wrong acquisition of things can be traded in and substituted with an obsession of "*stealing those who steal*" from the jaws of the activity — stealing. You would need their co-operation, (and this requires you earning their trust). Another example is encouraging students who are obsessed with cheating in their studies, to trade the cheating for learning. This is because the same mental intelligence required to cheat and succeed is the same that is required to study and succeed. The denominator here is to succeed, and the variable is the kind of activity involved.

However, if you are the one struggling with 'uncontrollable internalisation', there is hope. You can overcome it if you do not want it, or change it into a life transforming experience. Mine came in useful in 'composition classes', but I had to find how to manage it. It was a battle. Self-will is not enough to help overcome this obsession. As a child when I hear a positive story even if it is incomplete, I go ahead and complete it in my brain. The same happens when I am engrossed with a serial programme on TV. When the serial ends, as I go to bed my brain automatically completes the story for the next series.

I later found out that my conclusion is not necessarily the same as that of that of the scriptwriter, but was based on where I was and how I wanted the end to be. The scriptwriter however came from a different location (emotionally, spiritually, socially, and morally) and based on this, he drew his conclusion. This contended with my study time, I had to pray to God for guidance, and He helped me. This was how I made it through school. With God, I was able to bring it under control and transform it into a useful tool.

There are yet, housemates that hear strange voices occasionally. If you fall into this category, like me, then you must realise that the word of God is the final word. Remember to discard what you hear if it does not measure up with the word of God. Go back to the book of Genesis 3. In order words, any voice or conversation that threatens your peace should be reviewed thoroughly. 1st Cor. 14 vs.33, Romans 3vs.4. As you are aware, the devil operates through his own troops (demons, otherwise known as fallen angels). You must recognise that there are unheard voices that would try to talk you out of obeying God; they always work in opposition to every divine authority. They are natural deviants!

In essence, not every voice you hear is acceptable; some may even sound very appealing. You ought to let the word of God judge all that you hear. 2nd Corinthians 2 vs.11. It is also important to know that having the right conversation with the wrong people can lead to trouble. Eve had no business conversing with the serpent. God, being their ultimate authority, had given them an instruction, and the serpent, being one of their subjects, opposed the instruction. Genesis 3 vs.1-5.

Bearing this in mind, we see the need to identify these attributes early enough. You would be able to cover one another's backs and strengthen your team of housemates. What you do not see, or know, God may open their eyes to see or even give them the understanding you need to move to your next level. He may allow them cover territories you may never visit in your lifetime.
Proverbs 22vs.22-23.

However, there may be times when power is abused in the process of trying to integrate others; withdrawal of support is a way to control it. There is no point supporting others and destroying yourselves in the process. Your goal is to remain in the field of support.

If you are losing your fight, look out for the attributes and deal with them. If you have been overcoming your fight, you may want to assist others with theirs. If you have already won a fight, do not relax, there are still more to come.

6

OFFICIALS OF YOUR FIGHT

Ephesians 2 vs.19 *"Now, therefore, you are no longer strangers and foreigners, but fellow citizens with the saints and members of the household of God".*

To fight and win any battle, you need the right people. In wrestling or boxing matches, there are referees and other officials to ensure you stay by the rules. There are also spectators to cheer you on as you fight. In the same manner, you need experienced people to help you win in your fight for destiny. You also need inspiration from others periodically.

You need to be aware of the parties involved in the fight. The first person is you, the victor or victim (you need to decide who you would be). Obviously, you want to be a winner or the victor in your fight for destiny. This calls for you personally mastering the fight, knowing your place in it and what you can do personally to put yourself in the winning stance. From your home to work, from neighbourhood to societal gatherings and places of worship, from market to places of leisure, you need to identify your place and stand firm there. We would talk about this exclusively in a latter chapter.

More so, to overcome any of the challenges mentioned above, you as an individual need to be well positioned. Not standing well can make you stumble or fall. For several years, I struggled with my health, at times it was psychological and at other times it was simply a childhood disease. The most difficult one was overcoming mild fits of epilepsy. Paying attention to the general rules of staying well groomed mentally (positive thinking), eating and sleeping well checked this. Following the medical advice and spiritual advice also put me in good position to sustain good health.

There is also the contender of your destiny. It is the devil manifesting through illness (terminal or short-lived), spiritual depravity (moral decadence and the like), career or academic distress, relational set backs and family degradation. All these fight to ensure that you do not get the promised joy and fulfilment from God. They always creep in when and where you do not expect. The bible says the source of all afflictions; as listed above is sin. This exposes you to the wiles of the enemy. Genesis 3 vs.6-7. The thing to do after sinning is to repent, there is no point apportioning blames. The deed has been done. The next thing to do is to rise up, shake the dust off, and keep running towards the mark. Look at the fall of man in Genesis. While Adam and Eve were casting the blame net, God stepped in, addressed the situation, and immediately began working on the solution — the redemption of humanity.

The loving God begins to deal with your sin by covering your nakedness, i.e. the object that was exposed to enemy's attacks. It is what the enemy finds on you that makes him mock you. It is the anomaly in your life that he keeps bringing to your remembrance. Genesis 3 vs.21. In fact, I believe that the reason man was driven from the garden after redemption was for him to leave the environment of mockery — where the devil can remind him of his shame. May God drive you out of the environment where the devil made you fall, or where the devil can remind you of your nakedness in Jesus' name.

Then, there are your supporters who encourage you as you journey along in the path of your destiny. They also help re focus you where they think you have strayed away or deviated from the norm. This means you need to learn to tolerate the people that you meet regularly. You would also need to manage your housemates;. They may not all be pleasant, and the pleasant ones may not be pleasant always. While it is a bit easy to manage some, how about those whose behaviour you find extremely inundating and exhaustive. You achieve this by placing a demand on God for grace and ability, while managing your own challenges. You may say that it is easy to exclude them from your life, if that is a simple option for you. How about if this person happens to be a loved one (child, or relative)?

Would you pretend the challenge is not there, or would you be prepared to work with them (if you know that there is a solution)? Well that may be the only request God would demand from you, for Him to expand you. You never know. At times hidden in these children of God, whose behaviour is challenging, could lie your destiny. What you do for them could turn out to be the best thing you would achieve in your entire life. You never can tell. Ecclesiastes 9 vs.10.

Finally, there is God, the house of creativity; giving you creative ideas or winning strategy for your fight. The fight may be individual or corporate, and regardless of this, you would need divine help from above. Since God created man, He did not hide His intention to work with him. God wants to walk with you. God wants to work through you. God wants to use you as a channel to get to your housemates, especially the ones whose behaviour you find challenging. He wants you to co-operate with others in life, regardless of their abilities. As you walk with God, He would encourage you to be of help and advise you on where to seek help. Your support to others would go a long way in helping them identify their unique gift; and help trigger yours. This is the only way to gain fresh insights and alleviate the fears of growing up.

> God wants to walk with you. God wants to work through you.

Wake up, identify the traits and take charge in providing the appropriate control. Arise and let God know that you are capable of co-operating with others. Relax and watch God win the battles of your life.

7

SUPPORT AVAILABLE

Matthew 25 vs.40 *"And the King will answer and say to them, 'Assuredly, I say to you, inasmuch as you did it to one of the least of these my brethren, you did it to me".*

I n the previous chapter, we see that we all belong to God; the house of creativity, despite our different abilities and challenges. Most times God would support or help you through others. To support a person is to assist him in achieving the goal he set out to accomplish. Support can be vertical (from a higher or lower source) or horizontal (from peers, colleagues, and acquaintances). Whichever dimension it takes, it would entail the physical, the emotional, the psychological, and the spiritual. However, before we can embrace the support available, we must know where the fight is.

The fight may be to maintain a healthy lifestyle after being diagnosed with a horrible disease, or it may be to over come a serious illness. The fight could also be to get your child out of a mess or to ensure he does not fall into the mess. The fight could be to change the results you are getting from your academic or career endeavours. It could also be a fight for your marital destiny whether you are single and lonely at marriageable age, or your marriage is taking the turn for the worse. You may also be struggling with your christian development or simply facing bankruptcy. All these have the potential to leave you in a state of distress. Knowing the support available would put you in the position to reach out for help in overcoming the challenges you face.

Physical support is given where there is a physical challenge. Where the challenge is physical; **y**ou may experience bodily pains, because of accidents incurred due to distraction and clumsiness. Physical challenge could also manifest as a handicap and where this is the case, there are equipment and kits to sort this out.

More so, inability to communicate well is another physical challenge you may experience. Spoken or body language refers to the mode of communication between people. The brain serves as the platform from which all-internal messages are communicated to man. This means that man's ability to process information depends on a number of factors, both internal and external. Your ability or inability to communicate effectively with your housemates would determine the level of frustration that you experience. What you do not want to do, is give up on communicating. Where this happens, people stray away and sort themselves out their own way. The effect of this could be devastating to the environment they live in, if their solution is not in line with godly principles.

More so, I can remember an ineffective conversation I had, it was simple but it failed to communicate the message clearly. My recipient did not understand and the Holy Spirit later led me to put my intentions in writing. The Holy Spirit said, "When a person speaks, the listeners hear what they want to hear, based on their location — past, present and future". As I asked Him to explain, He said, "You are talking to people, who have past experiences, are in the middle of an experience today, and have certain expectations tomorrow". In addition, when you talk to people, you normally talk to them based on where you are now, in preparation for where you are going, using where you have been as a tool. This means that they would respond to you based on where they are (past, present, and future)".

This explains the reason why you should always pray to God to help you reach people where they are when you communicate with them. The songwriter, William .C. Burns, wrote the following verse of a hymn:

"Oh teach me Lord, that I may teach,
The precious things thou doth impact,
And wing my words that they may reach,
The hidden depths of many a-heart".

The emotional support deals with the feelings. Emotions are the feelings experienced as one interacts with life. Your experiences with life will usually trigger positive and negative emotions. These emotions would often lead to ideas in the mind, which only the spirit of God can bring out. 1st Corinthians 2vs.11. The bible also says the word of God is a discerner, able to reach the deepest parts of man. Hebrews 4vs12 tells us that the Holy Spirit is also the discerner. There is no part, depth, or height He cannot reach. In the case of emotional challenges, you may experience anxieties, worries, fears, unacceptable mood swings; a by-product of poor thinking habit picked up while meditating on wrong things. To be able to influence people sincerely, and get the right response, you may need to help them achieve emotional stability; with emotional intelligence. You cannot do it by manipulation, only God can sustain the support you give. Ecclesiastes 3vs.14.

A major emotional challenge you may face when relating with some housemates is their inability to comprehend the message you put across. You will need to pray for their understanding to be quickened by God. Job 32 vs. 8. Remember Abraham, the father of faith, He interceded for Lot, when he was captured. Now in the case of your housemates, their understanding may have been captured too and you may need to intercede for them. Genesis 14vs.12. This requires real love and some measure of sacrifice on your part. Abraham had to leave his comfort zone before he could rescue Lot. Genesis 14 vs.14-16.

The psychological support is given to aid the housemates with challenges in this area. We have identified obsession as one of the psychological challenges you may be experiencing. In my case, I was able to convert it into something positive. However, the fact that obsession can be useful does not mean that you should not address it. It can also be very destructive. It can make you drift, lose out on vital information and cause you to become a poor communicator. It can also lead to poverty, if not checked early. Where it is psychological, it may be also lead to anxiety; leading to fear (of future, rejection and failure).

More so, because the processing of information in some people's brain is a bit unusual, their responses would also be a bit unusual. Only a strong support systems and divine intervention can guarantee a successful life. You can support them by guiding their thought in the direction it has started heading; if is in the positive direction. This is where the word of God comes in. Hebrews 4 vs.12. Allow the word to pierce through their hearts, and like a sower, give it the opportunity to grow. Once the word is sown, you can then leave the rest to God. He will guide their thought life and protect them from drifting into a prodigal zone. This is the zone where cruelty and love is embraced. It is the spirit of God that would encourage good behaviour among your housemates.

The spiritual support is given to help combat spiritual challenge, which occurs, and influences behaviour positively or negatively. This is because man is a spirit being, and the world is influenced by so many spirits (both good and bad). You and your housemates would therefore act positively or negatively depending on the kind of spirit, that influences you all. So there fore, for you to influence them positively and bring about lasting change, you must go through God. For you to get to God, you must go through Jesus. John 14 vs. 6.

The social support is given to check social challenges. Social challenges are likely to occur every time you are, "absent" in the midst of people or are not aware of certain expectations or behaviours. Your absence means that they have nothing to respond to. Passing the ball o f conversation or expectations becomes hard and keeping track of the "game of socialising" becomes almost impossible. Obviously, this frustrates the server and he has the option of either passing the ball without receiving it or finding himself another playmate. The later option is usually embraced by the majority.

To conclude to this chapter, it would be important to note that you should not attempt to destroy what you cannot make. You cannot make yourself or your housemates, so please do not think of destroying yourselves. Release yourselves to God, He will break you, melt you, mould you, and fill you again. When He is done, He will give them back to you. 1st Samuel 1vs.28, 1st Samuel 7 vs.15. Hannah gave Samuel back to God, and God gave her more children and He gave Israel a priest.

Allow God, transform your life. Allow God use you to encourage others. Embrace the numerous supports available to you.

8

STRENGTHEN THE SUPPORT

Proverbs 3 vs.27 *"Do not withhold good from those to whom it is due when it is in your power to do it"*

Having considered the support available to you and your housemates, what happens where this is not enough? What you do here is to strengthen the support. How do you strengthen the support? It is only possible by reaching out for the appropriate help. As a member of the house of creativity, you can be assured that you are not alone in your struggles. Pray and ask God to lead you to those who would assist you. God may also lead others to you so you can help them. It may be the only assignment God has called you to perform. If you take up this challenge, be assured that, God would protect and look after your wellbeing, and that of your housemates. You do not have to feel helpless about the challenges. Commit yourselves to God, and He would keep you all from the enemy. John 10 vs.29.

More so, support can also be individual or corporate and this can be physical, emotional, psychological, social or spiritual. All these involve giving practical aid to a person in the course of fulfilling a task or purpose. This may mean getting involved with the dreams of others and helping to bring about its fulfilment. God may use this medium to open your eyes to see how you would achieve yours. What kind of help is available to you or your housemates?

Firstly, encouragement by communicating and active listening. This will improve your concentration skills, memory and ability to process information rightly. These tools are necessary, to avoid abortive effort. The purpose of the encouragement must be clearly understood — that is desire to support.

Secondly, you also need to establish a bond of trust. This you do by leading by example. A school of thought believes that some housemates do not understand clues. I dare to challenge that. Some may not, but most do, especially those who have retrained their senses. Indirect clues from you would receive indirect responses from them. Have you ever considered why you do not understand others or why they do not understand you? It may be the case of two separate minds relating to each other from separate positions. Where trust is desired, transparency must be encouraged. Live by example. When help is the goal, do not say one thing and mean another. Do what you say and say what you do.

Thirdly, you need to understand that the expected result of all support given, is to be guided in the right direction. This would require seeking help in an appropriate manner. Remember any one forced to move against God's will would ultimately rebel because the vulnerability of man opens them up for abuse. Successful negotiations in behavioural patterns can nudge people towards the desired path God has ordained for them. This is when you would be able to persuade and positively influence them.

More so, there are some institutions (like special schools for children and youths) already in place to meet further needs of some of our beloved housemates. As with every other human being, regardless of mannerism of learning, some of our housemates need a stable environment and some form of continuity. These can only be provided by a stable home and environment. More money is incurred in corrective measures. Prevent the damage and maintenance would be economical.

Where psychological support needs to be intensified, patience is important. Supporting yourself or your housemates may prove to be demanding and can be draining emotionally, and psychologically. The only way out is by asking God to brace you with the spirit of endurance and determination. Only the word of God can help people develop the right balance emotionally. Where this is lacking, there is a tendency for cruelty to manifest. The word of God is the gauge to measure actions.

2nd Corinthians 5 vs.14 *"For the love of Christ controls us . . . ."*

In addition, fear, pain, or boredom are psychological challenges that may make you or your housemates 'run away' mentally. Seeking God when this happens can help you develop the right emotional balance. You may not be able to control genuinely positive responses; you can only create the atmosphere for it and pray. We can see an example of this in the life of Abraham in Genesis 16. He loved Sarai, but did not really love Hagar. In fact, it was his love for Sarai that made him listen to her and sleep with Hagar. Genesis 16 vs.1-4. You may not be able to use a person, object or circumstance to make people do what you want (manipulate them). Although Hagar had a child for Abraham, when Sarah told him to send her away, with the child, he did. He grieved, he did not intercede. Genesis 21

How ever, whenever you find your housemate escaping reality, a good way to bring them back is to pray that God locates and re positions them. Hagar was fleeing from where she was supposed to be, when God found her. The angel of God located her *(even though she was not looking for God at that particular time)*. No matter where you are, the grace of God can locate and place you where you need to be (emotionally and mentally). Genesis 16 vs.6-11

More over, if you find out that you are the one that runs away emotionally or mentally, the same principles apply. Not only can God locate you, He will also bless you where He has ordained you to be. Do not run off in the face of the heat. Be present. Face the challenge, face the pain, face your emotions, and watch God help you develop the right emotional intelligence in every situation you find yourself. It is most likely that you are the one that would have the most influence on your housemates, because you would be closest to them. You need to remind them that everything God makes is very good; and becomes distorted when sin is introduced into it. Eve had a perfect identity in God until the devil distorted her view. Once the devil distorted Eve's image in her mind, he was able to manipulate her mind to disobey God.

How ever, when they make mistakes is not the time to crush their soul. Like every other person, if you do this you communicate to them that it is all right to be cruel. This is the time to admonish and encouraged them with the word of God. Let them know that like every other person, they would sin against God and man from time to time. This does not mean that they are bad people; it is the human nature playing up. As earlier stated, the thing to do after sinning is to repent.

There would also be times in the course of your interaction with your house mates, that you feel that you can no longer take it, remember Abraham, the father of faith in Genesis18. During the heat *(or a turbulent time)*, God appeared to him, he lifted up his eyes, and saw God. He was able to adjust his

> No matter where you are, the grace of God can locate and place you where you need to be (emotionally and mentally).

vision to be in God's direction. He knew he had seen God, because there was a witness in him. He might not have seen God if he had not lifted his gaze. In times of difficulty, align your gaze with God. **Genesis 18 vs.1-2.** It might take a while to see your housemates perform the way you expect them to, but consider Abraham and imitate him. Though the promise had not happened, Abraham still honoured God through his offerings. You do not need to wait for the manifestation of God's promises in their life, before you bless Him.

More so, blessing Him is a sign that you believe that He is able to do that which He said He would do in their lives. As you continue to serve and offer thanks to God on their behalf, God would continue to release His peace to you, during your waiting period. The offering Abraham gave provoked another confirmation of God's promise to him. Hebrews 11 vs.11. God did not make the mistake of announcing the promise to you. He does it, so you could draw nearer to Him, and learn to walk the paths that will eventually lead to the fulfilment of the promise.

Never doubt the promises of God even when it looks impossible. Never depart from His word, seen that it is the compass. Never fail to look to Him, seeing that is where the support is.

9

CYCLES OF FIGHT

Ephesian 6 vs. 13 'Wherefore take unto you the whole armour of God that ye may be able to withstand in the evil day, and having done all, to stand'.

Having mastered your person and your uniqueness, you also need to master your fight and rules of winning. There are fights that happen once in a lifetime, there are some that happen as you go through life, and there are some that occur in cycles. A cycle refers to a phase or sequence of events. It is a repetitive and recurring pattern. Some fights also tend to be recurring in their pattern. It could be in the form of a recurring illness, pattern of redundancy, after being offered a good job, or pattern of marital failures, e.t.c. All this are unpleasant cycles of change that can mar ones destiny.

A biblical example is found in Genesis; where there was a cycle of contention in Isaac's life over the wells his father had dug. God blessed him exceedingly in a foreign land. The indigenes saw it and envied him. His prosperous father; Abraham had dug certain wells, and the indigenes decided to fill it after the death of Abraham. Isaac needed the wells and everywhere he went there seem to be an unpleasant pattern of events. Those were Isaac's wrestle grounds. Whenever he began digging the wells, no one said anything, but as soon as the wells were dug, the opposition started. The pattern eventually ceased when God gave Isaac a breakthrough. He knew it was God's provision for him when the contention had ceased.

In your life, there is need to overcome any unpleasant recurring pattern, if you must win this fight for destiny. If

Isaac had not being persistent, he may never have succeeded in getting his own Rehoboath. My fight was once extreme internalisation. It was not an easy fight to overcome. I can assure you that if you are caught in this, overcoming it is not going to be a smooth ride, with you seating, folding your arms and smiling all the way. Infact that is the easiest way to drift from your goal. You need to work out your mode of survival and sustain it. For Apostle Paul in the bible, he had to press in to achieve his purpose. Despite his handicap, status and the people's resistance and opinion, he ran with one mind. He was committed and focus in his responsibility to God after his conversion. With God's encouragement, he prospered, he was able to take charge of his life, and manage his brethren. You need to be persistent in the face of the battle.

More so, mastering your fight requires you being alert. There are certain patterns that when you experience them, you need to break them immediately. Usually you do this through the word and through prayers. The times in my life when I fall into unpleasant cycles, I remember that *'every thing can be broken, only the scriptures cannot be broken'* and I begin to use the word. It is also important to know where the cycles of fight take place. In the case of Isaac, the cycles of fight was in the fields where he dug the wells. In your life, it could be trying to pass an examination, after experiencing series of failures, trying to sustain a pregnancy after series of abortions, trying to break free from drug addictions, trying to overcome a recurring illness e.t.c. Whatever cycle you are experiencing today, remember, it can be broken. The word of God cannot be broken, so definitely, the unpleasant cycle in your life has to be broken and it would break in Jesus' name.

The cycles of your fight could come from friends, close associates or even acquaintances. There are yet some cycles that occur across generations. It may be a particular illness from a father to his children, or a pattern of sins running down the family line. Over the years, God has blessed researchers and certain diseases that were thought in times past to be incurable are now curable.

In addition, patterns of death in some families (due to unknown illnesses) have now being terminated, with discoveries and the cure for the illnesses. Amongst tribes and nations, there are patterns of cycles that are broken with God's intervention. For example, all through the Old Testament, the bible's record of Israel, after they fell was '. . . . and they called on God, and God heard them' or 'sent a man to rescue them'. As expected as one generation gave way to the next, some children of Israel sinned against God, and God allowed the devil to afflict them. When they realised their sin, they repented and God heard them. This tells me without doubt that the cycle of discomfort in your life can also be broken in Jesus' name.

Arise; identify the fight in your life. Fight the good fight of faith. Trust in God as you watch Him break the cycle.

10

OVERTHROW THE GIANT

Galatians 5 vs.26 *"Let us not become conceited, provoking one another, envying one another"*.

As you begin to expand your territory and accommodate others, there are giants that usually appear on the scene. A giant is an enormous entity that tends to intimidate the mind. It is also a colossal entity that challenges the human mind. It may be a positive concept as seen in the building structures and illusions we have today, and it could be a negative ideology, leading to fallacy. What is the giant in your own life that you must overthrow to win the fight for destiny? There are times when these giants come in because of the people in your life; your housemates may have opened the door for them. The giants come through seemingly harmless events like thoughts and actions that induce fear, anxiety, sickness, rejection or even failure. They may also come to hinder your growth, and scare you off your goals. If you let them in, they can mar your destiny.

In addition they roar from within (home, and close associates) to the external world (society, community or even nation). The result they leave behind is oppression, obsession, possession and affliction. Their roaring can be very discomforting. The bible says that 'the devil is like a roaring lion'. We thank God because we know that 'Jesus Christ is the lion of the tribe of Judah' — the king of the jungle. Revelations 5 vs.5. The devil is a lion, but Jesus is the king of all lions, the unequalled one. It does not matter where these giants are roaring from, with God, you cannot go wrong. You are not alone. Remember, Goliath in the days of David; the shepherd boy. 1ˢᵗ Samuel 17vs. 23.

The monstrous guy roared morning and evening; in the ears of Israel until they became distressed. Israel's cry came up to God and the spirit of God moved David and gave him a wining idea that brought the head of Goliath down eventually. You need to have faith in God and believe that every Goliath in your life has elapsed their tenure.

More over, if you refuse to follow God's leading to overthrow the giant, you would have disobeyed Him. You must withstand the giant. Withstand the devil (giant) and he would flee. The giant in your life comes as you become aware of your consciousness. In the life of a child, the giant can come in because of neglect from birth, bullying at school or even malnutrition. As a young adult, it may come from effects of wrong associations, wrong paradigms and unrealistic expectations and demands. The giant if not checked can continue roaring into your adult life. Some people have allowed the giants to kill them in the process of neglecting it or handling it poorly. This is not God's will. His will is for you to win the fight for your own destiny.

What is the giant in your own life that you must overthrow to win the fight for destiny? One of the biggest ones you would come across in your life is the giant of self. If you can successfully confront this giant, you would usually win the fight for your destiny. Constantly confronting this giant helps you serve and support people, regardless of who you are or what they intend to achieve.

More so, in every thing you do, your motive should be to please God. You or your housemates may be bare — intellectually, or financially, with no sign of creativity. You may not be a painter, writer, artist, e.t.c. Your ability to be productive may also be latent and may require a bit of steering up. What you need to realise is that God can use you for whatever He wants, when He wants and how He wants. Proverbs 19 vs.21. Whatever He has called you to do, you need to trust and obey Him. It may not always be easy to fight that inner giant called self. For example, if you have to be a cheerleader; leading others on into glory, or even fire fighters; settling disputes and challenges that occur, you would need to forget about that giant of self. It all depends on God, and the ability He has put in you.

In Genesis 11, the people in Babel embarked on a selfish motive, they wanted to build for themselves, and God did not prosper the work of their hands. In the same vein, if you would succeed at co-operating with God to accommodate your housemates, your motives have to be pure. It must be hinged on guiding them in achieving God's purpose. From the passage in Genesis 11, one could think that God is against unity. The interesting thing is God is the one who weighs the heart, so He would know if your motives are pure or not. God will not encourage people with the wrong motives. He will ensure that plans outside His will are frustrated. Every potential leader (housemate) raised outside His will invariably become perverse. Pure motives however, would invariably attract His blessings. Psalm 133 vs. 1-3, Galatians 5 vs.26.

A biblical example of a person that overcame the giant of self was Ruth. It must have been a challenge to accommodate (cope with) Naomi. Ruth did not have to; because everything that brought them together, (her husband and children) were dead. Ruth 1 vs.16. Naomi must have had a challenging behaviour during her trial period because after tragedy struck; she heard of what God was doing in the midst of her people and decided to go and partake of it alone. She did not bother inviting her daughters in-law. Ruth 1 vs.6.

> *The culture you embrace can only take you as far as the area it covers. How well you respect the culture you find yourself determines how well the people would receive you.*

On getting home, people came to rejoice with her, but she could not reciprocate the joy, she did with sarcasm. Ruth 1 vs.19. She changed her name because of her circumstances. She labelled herself and instructed every one to join her in agreeing with her circumstance, rather than agreeing with God. Ruth 1 vs.20. She became a grumbler, murmuring against God. Ruth 1 vs.21.

However, Ruth, a loyal girl was willing to accommodate her mother in − law, despite her challenging behaviour. She was also willing to accommodate the culture (godly) she found herself. The culture you embrace can only take you as far as the area it covers. How well you respect the culture you find yourself determines how well the people would receive you. Ruth was rewarded for aligning herself with God and allowing Him use her as a vessel to assist Naomi. She became the bride of the wealthiest man around. Not a bad reward after all! Favour is not fair, but it is not cheap either. There is always a price for it.

Overcome that giant. Get rid of that Me. Loose yourself for God's favour.

11

MAINTAIN YOUR STANCE

Romans 16vs.19-20 *"Be excellent at what is good, be innocent of evil, and the God of peace would soon crush satan underneath your foot.*

In the course of overthrowing the giants in your life, you need to be patient. Some giants leave immediately while others do not. For the ones that persist, the word of God encourages you to persevere in doing good to yourself and your housemates. To maintain your stance is to hold a good posture and carriage wherever you find your self and in whatever circumstance you find yourself. It is to have a good disposition to life. Occasionally you may lose your stance, and fall, but through the grace of God, you would rise again in Jesus' name. Goliath persisted in the life of Israel, but God eventually gave Israel the victory.

Biblical examples of others who also maintained their stance during the fight for destiny includes Daniel in the lion's den; Daniel 6vs. 20, and Shadrach, Mesach, and Abednego in the fiery furnace. Daniel 3vs.26. We see Jesus Christ maintaining His stance in the face of temptation as well. Matthew4vs.11. In maintaining your stance, there may be times when you would need God, like Daniel, and some times, like Moses; you would need people; like Aron and Hur lifting up your hands. In order words, you may need your housemates to maintain your stance. It is part of striving for excellence at what is good.

With the support mechanism in place, and your housemates' co-operation, you can maintain your stance. In the normal event of life, accountability is required of all living things, especially man. Once a person has been assisted to a certain level, he is expected to go forth and multiply (reproduce). The same principle applies to your housemate. Once they have been supported to an extent, they should be encouraged to launch out. You would need to maintain your stance (to achieve victory) everywhere you find yourself. Where your housemates seem impossible, the spirit of God is available to help you love them.

More so, the spirit of God can inspire and encourage them to launch out, regardless of the challenges they face. Imagine the joy of a mentor whose "deaf pianist" produces outstanding musical pieces (like Ludwig van Beethoven), or a maimed (hand and feet) housemate, who can paint so well with his mouth, like Steve Chambers. Better still, imagine a housemate who has been classified, as mentally retarded, and he suddenly becomes an excellent scholar! What a thrill for the mentors (parents, guardians and friends)! All these can be possible by nurturing the latent potentials for God. Colossians 3vs.12-13.

It is not God's plan that any of his children become a burden. What ever you do for them, you are doing it for God. He intends every one of His children (your housemates inclusive) to fulfil their purpose before leaving the world. Everyone is sent to the earth on a mandate, so maintain your stance in the fight.

In God's original design, no one is irrelevant. My mum, while in business always believed that 'no one is irrelevant. Every one has a purpose". Guess what? She never had problems managing people! I am of the opinion that this is the truth she held onto that made me want to be like her. Take your stance with your house mates. They need to be made comfortable in the world created by you. Pull them into your world, and let them help you transform your world to

> It is not God's plan that any of his children become a burden.

unimaginable levels of advancement — a habitable place for you and them. Catch them young, hold the grown ups close and care for the elderly. It is not going to be an easy task, but it is going to be worth it. Colossians 3vs.17.

If your call in life is to work with special needs, successfully communicating the love of God to your housemates may also help you in maintaining your stance. This would help them hold on in the face of negativity when they eventually launch out into the public. You may discover that these housemates are normal, they only learn in a different way from their colleagues. Job 32 vs.8. There may also be times in trying to maintain your stance that you may need to understand and challenge normalcy. What is normal? Normal is relative in life. Who decides or determines what is normal? Life operates on the principle of the majority. If normal behavioural determinant is left in the hands of man, who changes from time to time, then normal must be relative.

A normal behaviour is therefore one that has been accepted over a period as adding value to man and his environment. Like a baton in a relay race, this pattern has been tried, tested, and proven over the years and from one generation to the next. The need to bridge the gap between the generally acceptable and the newly discovered acceptable has made science come up with intermediaries. You may be one of those who take their stance in the fight of life by living in two worlds — the common and the uncommon; trained to put yourself in the shoes of others. The interesting thing is that both worlds have their struggles, and your ability to integrate these worlds together goes a long way in achieving common goals.

Part of maintaining your stance may be to monitor your housemates as they go into the world. They may feel vulnerable and require additional help in a world that had not considered them until recently. Awareness of this vulnerability may not be there in the early years, until they get older and discover that they do things differently. The knowledge of God's love and their uniqueness (impacted to them from their early days) would help them maintain their stance and overcome any challenge that they would later face in life. Monitor from a distance to prevent them from going off tangent. When people go off tangent, perverseness may set in. A biblical example of this is the children of Benjamin in Judges 20-21. For some strange reasons, they became perverse. It took the grace of God for them to be restored (remain among the twelve tribes of Israel). Judges 21 vs. 3, Judges 21 vs.17. As earlier said, it is the joy of a mentor is to see his protégée succeed and people come back to say, "Thank you".

Imagine how Naomi must have felt, after Ruth delivered a baby and the whole city rejoiced with her. Notice, the bible did not say they rejoiced with Ruth (although they would have). The bible said that they rejoiced with Naomi. Ruth 4 vs.14-15. Let us analyse the success here. Ruth engineered her success, and Naomi supported her, through mentoring. Ruth carried endured the pregnancy and went through pain to deliver the baby and Naomi got the praise. Ruth delivered the baby, Naomi nursed him, and the society got the joy of naming the baby, whose lineage was going to produce the saviour, our Lord Jesus Christ. Ruth 4 vs.16-17.

A good restoration for the protégée (Ruth). A good reward for Naomi (her mentor). A good legacy for their lineage (the future).

12

THE INEVITABLE – YOUR VICTORY CHANT

Psalms 47 vs.5 'God is gone up with a shout, the LORD with the sound of a trumpet'.

You have seen that by taking charge of your life, you can maintain your winning stance in the fight. The Apostle Paul testified to the fact that God indeed gave you a gift (treasure), to be all that you can be. If you consider God's power, and His willingness to support you, you would be amazed at how much He can achieve through you. 2nd Corinthians 4 vs.7-9. One thing that I have been silent about until now is the ultimate destiny enhancer for everyone. Without it, every other thing would fail. Eight five percent of the times that I refused to continue with the fight for destiny, the scent of it spurned me on. It is the victory chant.

The victory chant is an appreciative response to a kind gesture or benefit received. Every one is entitled to it, but few take advantage of it. It is an aroma given off as you praise and give thanks to God. I have been in positions in life where I either had to live, move or work with housemates in challenging conditions. Praise and thanksgiving solved what was seemingly impossible. We need the victory chant to set our spirit free. When I had frozen tears, the sound (no matter how faint) of the victory chant thawed the tears, and allowed them flow down my cheeks; receiving God's comfort. The times I was prayed up stiff, the chant of anticipated victory loosened the blood, and I felt the free flow of blood through my veins. In times of anxiety and fear of the next moment, the scent of the victory chant pulled me up, and opened my eyes to the next step to take in life. Philippians 4 vs. 6-7.

More so, to attain your victory chant, you may need your housemates, regardless of their behaviour because the pattern God gave us is to love people, regardless of their actions. This was what He did. Romans 5vs.8. Victory chant introduces an atmosphere of gratitude that influences good behaviour; needed to sustain your victory in the fight for destiny. When you do not know which way to turn, victory chant can open you to new perspective. Look at the wall of Jericho. Joshua 6 vs.20. As Israel gave the shout of victory, the oppressive walls came down. It did not make sense to match round the wall quietely for six days and on the seventh day let out the noise. Israel could have given the excuse for not doing so and the oppression could have continued. Thank God they did.

Like Israel, you can also have an excuse for behaving either bad or good. It does not take being a genius to give an excuse for unacceptable behaviour. The question is this, do you want an excuse to be right or wrong. Your answer to this question determines how well you position yourself for victory. In order words, you can choose a victory stance, regardless of how other people act. Like good behaviour, an attitude of gratitude or victory chant is a choice.

Your housemates may also want to decline the invitation to partake of the victory chant. Let them see the reason why victory is eminent. For example, there is "a reason they have to know God as their best friend, rather than hanging out with "bullies" or "preys". There is a reason why they must seek help from appropriate quarters, rather than isolating themselves, until they become suicidal". There is also a reason why they have to ensure that they achieve godly success at all cost, no matter what they see, hear, or know about their past". In the bible, Judas had a reason to betray Jesus. He wanted fame among the chief priests and scribes. Matthew 26 vs. 47. He

> Everyone can have an excuse for behaving either badly or good.

could not have been in need, Jesus must have seen to that. No one can follow Jesus genuinely and be in need. Zechariah 10 vs.1, Matthew 7 vs.11. What he wanted was to be reckoned with, amongst the rulers of his time.

What he did not know however was the fact that they were only using him. The world does not love genuinely. Any love aside of God's love is false, and would erode with the passage of time. The love the world knows is the type of love that uses people and dumps them like thrash. It is the love that always seeks to get, without thinking of giving. Matthew 27 vs.3-4.

More so, to receive the spirit that provokes the victory chant, you must value your self. The value you place on yourself will be the value others would place on you. You cannot demand from people what you have not given to yourself. As a child of God, you must never lower the standards you set for yourself. You were purchased with the blood of Jesus. This is the ultimate price anyone can ever pay for you. Do not settle for less. This is the message you must also communicate to your housemates as well. 1st Corinthians 6 vs.20. In Eden, man sold his freedom and birthright to the devil, and God bought them back with the blood of Jesus. Do not sell yourself cheap, if the devil wants you back; assess the price he is willing to pay for you (it can never be more than the blood (of Jesus) that was shed for you). Judges 13 vs.7-8, Judges 16 vs.30, Luke 1 vs.13-17, Matthew 14 vs. 8-12.

More over, the fact that you started the battle with God does not mean that you would win the fight for destiny. You need to continue with God and let Him lead the way to your victory. Both Samson and John the Baptist operated under powerful anointing, but both had a tragic end. Why? Did they take their battles for granted or did they try their best, but the devil prevailed? Could they have done better? Against all odds, did their faith fail them along the way and they forgot the God of their battles?

However, one thing we should bear in mind is this every battle in your life is an opportunity to invite God to demonstrate His power. For the few in the bible whose destinies were tragic, there were many who had fruitful endings. Examples of these include Abraham, Isaac, Jacob, Moses, Joshua, Enoch, Samuel, Elijah, Jesus Christ, John the revelator, e.t.c. For many of these, it is not so much as how they lived, but how well they fought their battles to achieve their purpose.

Finally, it is my true desire to see you all in heaven at the end of our fights for destiny and hear God say to us; 'well done good and faithful servant, enter into the rest of the Lord . . .' Remember God completed His work in you, regardless of who you are. He made you a paragon of excellence, and all you have to do is co-operate with Him. Let the Almighty God; the definition of strength, the beginning and the end of power, and the Encapsulation of Destiny, use you to reach your housemates from the "House of Creativity'.

People may not have supported you in the preparation for battle, but by leaning on God, He can support you to victory. People may not have strengthened you in the fight for your destiny, but God would keep His hand on you until you get the victory, if you invite Him. People's strength may not amount to much, but as you seek the Lord in His strength, you would not go wrong.

CONCLUSION

Psalm 37 vs. 5 *"Commit your way to the Lord, trust also in Him, and He shall bring it to pass"*.

If you think that time is not on your side and that you have have lost the battles in your life, do not worry, at least you are still alive. As long as you have the breathe of God (life), there would be opportunities for God to demonstrate His power in your life. It is never too late to fight for your destiny. You can start now. The most important one is the fight to make heaven. If you are on your dying bed, that is a good one to fight for. If you are not yet there, you can fight to leave a positive landmark; let someone thank God that you came along. Put a smile on someone's face.

In addition, the covenant keeping God (source of all support) is looking for a generation that would take up the Abrahamic covenant, seal it with the Messianic covenant, run with it, and project it, so that His glory will be manifest in that generation.

The generation that refuses to acknowledge God's leadership and sovereignty, will lose the fight to see His glory.

Remember God is the source of your existence, the embodiment of your future, the house of creativity, and the encapsulation of your destiny. He created you to relate with others from various works of life; upholding the good and denouncing evil. He expects you to promote the one house principle amongst your housemates, and fight to see one another succeed. Make sure you fight for a purposeful living; possessing all the divine power God said is possible for you and laying hold on your inheritance; guaranteed by the Holy Spirit. Lastly, since the venues of these fights are not usually known, as most fights are spontaneous, make sure you are well prepared. God bless you.

Arise, discover and begin to celebrate your uniqueness in God. Arise, prepare for battle and begin to fight for your destiny. Arise, maintain your praise stance and begin to chant your way to victory.

A prayer to encourage you; a leader or a follower: to stay in the place of your call, and fight

*A*s the olive tree gives oil, with which men honour one another and God, So will your service give oil, which will honour man and God.

*A*s the fig tree, gives sweetness, and good fruit, so will your life give sweetness to man and God

*A*s the vine gives new wine which cheers man and God, So will your life continue to release service, which will cheer man and God,

*A*s the bramble gives shelter and shade to man, so will the spirit enable your service to protect those whom God would commit to your care.

*A*men.

Judges 9 verse 8-15